Believing in God

To Kyle and Kirsty

Published by
The Bible Reading Fellowship
Peter's Way, Sandy Lane West
Oxford OX4 5HG
ISBN 1 84101 104 5

First edition 2000
10 9 8 7 6 5 4 3 2 1 0

Acknowledgments
Scripture quotations are taken from the Good News Bible
published by The Bible Societies/HarperCollins*Publishers* Ltd UK
© American Bible Society, 1966, 1971, 1976, 1992.

A catalogue record for this book is available from the British Library.

Printed and bound in Great Britain by Caledonian International
Book Manufacturing Ltd, Glasgow.

Beginning with God

Believing in God

Exploring the Bible with 5-7s

Rachel Heathfield

A note to parents and carers

This material is to be used ideally with some help. It is designed to help you to talk to your child about God-things and to learn together.

Every session begins with an idea for looking back at the day and thinking of something or someone in particular. That thing or person is then to be prayed for. Encourage your child to voice their prayer, even if it is just a name or word.

The next bit is to enable you to talk together about a topic which will help you to understand what the Bible verse of the day is about. There are no right or wrong answers here, simply ideas to get you thinking on the right lines. Do not be afraid of difficult questions your child might raise; just be as honest as you can.

There is always a suggestion of something to do, which varies from matching up pictures to organizing a time to get up and see the sunrise. This section is deliberately worded so that the activity doesn't have to happen at that moment—particularly if you do the sessions at bed-time! Please support your child by helping him or her to do the activity, and give a reminder of why that activity was suggested.

Explore the Bible is designed to bring together the talking and doing you have just worked through. It might raise more questions, and the answers should be made easier by referring back to the talking bit.

The last part of the session is for the child to complete their own prayer journal on the pages provided. Each session has a linked thought and prayer suggestion. Again, this can be completed straightaway or at another time. Some children might need help; others might like to do it on their own.

I hope you enjoy this material, and may God bless the time you spend with your child exploring the Bible together.

Rachel Heathfield

Faith is...

Looking back

Think of the people you spend a lot of time with. Why do you like them?

Thank God for friends. Ask him to be a friend to lonely people.

To talk about

Have you got a video recorder? If you haven't, do you know someone who has?

What do you use a video recorder for? If you were going out and your favourite programme was on TV, what could you do? Does the machine always do what it is asked to do? How do you know it's going to work while you are out?

To do

There are lots of things that we do, trusting that they will work even though we don't actually see them in action. Here are some examples. What do we trust to happen?

Explore the Bible

> **To have faith is to be sure of the things we hope for, to be certain of the things we cannot see.**
>
> *Hebrews 11:1*

God is a bit like the things we use that we trust will work.

We talk to him when we pray, but we can't see him listening. We believe that he will do what he says, but we can't see him in action. We ask him to help us, but we don't actually see him doing those things. We have faith and trust that even though we can't actually see God, he will listen, do what he says, and help us.

Prayer jotter

Having faith in God is having confidence that although we don't see him nod or shake his head, we know deep inside that he is saying 'yes' or 'no'.

Is it easy to have faith in God? Do you trust him to be with you? Write or draw a prayer here.

Noah's faith

Looking back

What did you do the last time you were at school?

Thank God for something great.

Thank God for something new.

Tell him about something not so good.

To talk about

Have you ever had to make a decision when lots of people were listening to you?

Have you ever given an answer to a question at school when everyone else disagreed with you? Have you ever spoken up saying one thing when lots of people were saying something else?

What would it feel like to be saying 'yes' to something when everyone else was saying 'no'?

To do

On the next page is a picture of the ark Noah built and some of the animals. If you want to read the story in full, it is in the first book of the Bible, Genesis, chapters 7 and 8.

Explore the Bible

It was faith that made Noah hear God's warnings about things in the future that he could not see. He obeyed God and built a boat in which he and his family were saved.

Hebrews 11:7

In the story of Noah and his ark, God told Noah that there was going to be a flood and he needed to build a boat to save his family and the animals. Noah trusted that God was right. Everyone else was saying, 'No, of course there won't be a flood', but Noah said 'yes' because he had faith in what God was saying to him. He couldn't see for sure that there was going to be a flood, but he believed God was right.

Prayer jotter

Sometimes, believing that God is right is a hard thing to do, especially if your friends don't believe in God.

Sometimes people are nasty to us for saying we believe in God. Write about it or draw it here if this has happened to you.

Abraham's faith

Looking back

Have you done anything naughty in the last few days? Do you think it upset anyone? Did it upset God?

Tell him about it and say sorry to him.

To talk about

Think about what it feels like to want something very much but not be able to have it.

Perhaps you know someone who has had a baby? Was it really good news for them?

Some people have always wanted to have a baby but they haven't been able to. Some people can't have a baby because their bodies have something wrong; some people can't have a baby because they are too old. Often this makes them sad.

To do

Here are some children who have got what they were promised. How do you think they feel?

Explore the Bible

It was faith that made Abraham able to become a father, even though he was too old and Sarah herself could not have children. He trusted God to keep his promise.

Hebrews 11:11

God had promised Abraham a large family. He had said that Abraham would have so many relatives it would be impossible to count them.

Why, then, were he and his wife Sarah still childless? Sarah couldn't have babies and Abraham was too old. But Abraham was sure that God would make him a father. He trusted God. And God did give him a child—a boy called Isaac. You can read about Abraham, Sarah and Isaac in Genesis, chapter 21.

Prayer jotter

Sometimes we want something that won't be very good for us.

Think about the things you ask God for. Are they sometimes things that are bad for you? Are they things you don't really need?

Talk, draw and pray about it now.

Week 1
Session 4

Moses' faith

Looking back

Who needs God's help at the moment? Tell their name to God.

Who needs God's love at the moment? Tell their name to God.

To talk about

What is the most difficult thing you have ever done? What is the scariest thing you have ever done? Were they the same things?

How did it feel before you did it? Did anyone encourage you to do it? Was anyone there making you feel safe?

Explore the Bible

It was faith that made Moses leave Egypt without being afraid of the king's anger.

Hebrews 11:27

Moses was the leader of God's people, the Israelites. He knew that they needed to leave the country where they were being kept as slaves—a country called Egypt.

God had told Moses to lead the people out of Egypt. Moses knew that the king of Egypt would be very cross if he did that. But Moses had faith that God would help him and keep his people safe. He trusted that God would look after his people and make something scary easier to do.

To do

Here are some scary things. Which would you do? Which would you not do?

Prayer jotter

Is there anything that really scares you? Is it something God might be able to help you with? Part of that help might be for you to talk to an adult you trust about it.

Draw it and pray to God asking for his help. Have faith that he will help you.

The Israelites' faith

Looking back

Look at the things you have that belong to you.

Some children don't have very many things. Pray for God to be with them. Thank him for your things.

To talk about

Think again about the difficult and scary things you thought about in the last session.

Were you thinking 'What if...?' about something to do with it? Maybe you were thinking something would go wrong.

What convinced you that it would be OK? Were you OK?

Explore the Bible

> It was faith that made the Israelites able to cross the Red Sea as if on dry land.
>
> *Hebrews 11:29*

When the people of Israel escaped from Egypt with Moses, they faced something very scary. They had to get across to the other side of a sea. How could they do that? God told Moses to hold out his stick over the sea. An amazing thing happened. God made the water divide and make a path through the middle.

The people might have looked at the path and said, 'What if the water comes back?' or 'What if we don't get all the way across?' But they didn't. They had faith that God would keep them safe as they crossed the sea.

To do

Here is a picture for you to colour of the people of Israel going through the path in the middle of the sea.

Prayer jotter

God wants to help us with our 'what if...' questions about life. He wants us to feel safe in his care and sure of his love for us.

Thank him for caring for you, using this space.

Gideon's faith

Looking back

What was the best bit in your day just gone?

Tell God about it, thanking him for it.

To talk about

What is the silliest thing you have ever done? What is the funniest thing you have ever done? Why did you do it? Was anyone else doing that silly or funny thing?

Have you ever done something because someone told you to, even though you weren't sure why?

To do

Have you ever had hiccups? There are lots of silly ideas for curing hiccups. Here are some of them. Have you ever tried any of them? Do they work?

Explore the Bible

It was faith that made the walls of Jericho fall down after the Israelites had marched round them for seven days.

Hebrews 11:30

The people of Israel needed to win a battle against the people of Jericho. In those days, when one army went to fight another, they would face each other on a field and then charge!

For this battle, though, God had told his people a way to win. But it seemed like a silly idea! They had to walk round the walls of the city for seven days and then blow on their trumpets. God promised them that the walls would fall down.

Even though it seemed silly, they did it and the walls did come down. They had faith that God was right.

God wants us to obey him and do what he asks. Sometimes we don't understand why he is asking us to do something, but if we believe God we must do as he asks.

Prayer jotter

God asks us to pray, to go to church, to love those who are nasty to us, to be kind to others…

Can you think of more? Do you think any of these things are silly? Draw or write about obeying God here.

I am with you

Looking back

Some people don't have a home to go to. This means that they sleep outside. They need help from people to find a home. Pray that God will help the helpers to do a good job.

To talk about

Has anyone promised you anything recently? What was it? Who promised you? Why did they promise it?

Are you looking forward to it happening? How do you know it will happen?

To do

Here are some promises. Have you ever heard them said? By whom?

- I promise I'll be there for when you come out…
- I promise I will help you with your maths…
- I promise I will talk to your teacher about it…
- I promise you can have a party for your birthday…

Explore the Bible

> **Remember that I have commanded you to be determined and confident! Don't be afraid or discouraged, for I, the Lord your God, am with you wherever you go.**
>
> *Joshua 1:9*

God made a promise to his people and to their leader, a man named Joshua. He promised that he would always be with them. Because God had promised that, it meant that Joshua was able to be determined and confident.

Joshua needed to be sure that God would be with him through the difficult times of being a leader. God was with Joshua. God keeps his promises.

Prayer jotter

God wants you, like Joshua, to be determined and confident. This is because God promises to you, as well as to Joshua, that he will be with you wherever you go.

Draw a picture of what you think you might be when you are older. Thank God that he will still be with you then as he is now.

Week 2
Session 2

You are special

Looking back

Do you know someone who is really old?

Pray that God will be with them and give them all they need.

To talk about

Do you have favourite things? Maybe a teddy, or a doll, or a special toy? Why do you like them so much? What do you do with that thing?

Do you have special people? What do you do for them that shows that you think they are special?

To do

Here are a few ways in which we show that people or things are special to us.

Which do you do? What else is there to do?

Explore the Bible

The Lord takes pleasure in his people.

Psalm 149:4

This verse tells us that God thinks we are very special. He looks at us and thinks we're great. He enjoys knowing us, just as we enjoy our special people and special things.

God shows that he enjoys us by loving us and taking care of us. He promises that he takes pleasure in us and he does, because God keeps his promises.

Prayer jotter

When God looks at you, he sees a special person who is wonderfully made and gorgeous.

Do you believe God's promise that he takes pleasure in you?

Draw yourself in the mirror here.

I love you

Looking back

What is the most beautiful thing you have ever seen? Thank God for eyes.

What is the most beautiful sound you've heard? Thank God for ears.

Your ears or eyes might not work very well. If so, pray that God will show you his world in a different way.

To talk about

When have you heard people say they love something? What do you say you love?

Is it only people or is it lots of things? I love… ice-cream. I love… dogs and cats.

Have you seen people on the TV saying they love someone? Is it a good thing to love someone? What does it mean you do for them?

Explore the Bible

'The mountains and hills may crumble, but my love for you will never end.' So says the Lord who loves you.

Isaiah 54:10

God says that he will love us for ever. God who made the whole universe and keeps it going loves each one of us… for ever. Isn't that amazing?

'I love you' means 'I will stay with you, care for you, protect you and want good things for you.' Sometimes people aren't very good at all that.

When God says, 'I love you', it is a perfect love. God will always love us because he keeps his promises.

To do

Here is an 'I love you' card from God to you. Colour it in and, when you feel sad or lonely, remember the words and repeat them in your head.

Prayer jotter

When someone loves us, we usually love them as well. If God loves you, do you love him back?

Just as we trust that God will look after us, so too we have faith that God loves us.

Write or draw about what it is like to be loved by God.

He gave us his Son

Looking back

Telling untruths and being unkind to others makes God sad.

Is there anything you have done in the day just gone that made God sad? Say sorry to him now.

To talk about

Think about the people at home who love you. What do they do for you to show you they love you? Think of all the jobs they do, all the things they give you, and all the ways they make sure you are OK.

If they are with you now, talk to them about how much they do for you and how much they love you.

To do

Here are some gifts that people give to show that they love each other. Match up the gifts with the people.

Explore the Bible

For God loved the world so much that he gave his only Son, so that everyone who believes in him may not die but have eternal life.

John 3:16

God loves us very, very much. He loves us so much that he gives us presents.

Not flowers or toys or diamonds, but something worth a lot more. He gave us his Son, Jesus, as a present. We need Jesus to sort out the mess that we make of our lives. He also gives us the gift of eternal life. This means that when we die, we will go to heaven and be there with God and Jesus.

Those are amazing gifts for God to give, but he will give them because God keeps his promises.

Prayer jotter

Thank God that he gives such amazing love-gifts.

Write about or draw your thoughts here.

New earth and heaven

Looking back

What is the thing you love to do the most? When will you do it again?

Thank God for the times you have done it and thank him for the times you can look forward to.

To talk about

Who lives near you? Who is the nearest?

What are they like? Are they good neighbours? What is good about living near other people?

Explore the Bible

Then I saw a new heaven and a new earth. Now God's home is with human beings! He will live with them, and they shall be his people. God himself will be with them and he will be their God.

Revelation 21:1 and 3

God promises that one day he will make a new earth and a new heaven. It will be amazing and perfect in every way. One of the most amazing things about this new heaven and earth is that God will be living there with us, as close as the people who live as our neighbours now. We will be God's neighbours! Isn't that amazing to think of?

This will happen. We can look forward to it, because God keeps his promises.

To do

What do you think the new heaven and earth will look like? What will it be like to have God as your neighbour?

Can you imagine what God's house will be like? Try to draw it on your prayer jotter.

Thank God for the promise of a new heaven and a new earth.

Thank him that in this new place he will be so close to us.

Prayer jotter

I think God's house will be like this…

No more tears

Looking back

Think about your friends. Why do you like them?

Thank God for the things you do together. Pray for anything a friend might need or is worried about.

To talk about

What makes you cry? What makes other people cry? When did you last cry? What was it about?

Do you know anyone who is ill? Do you know anyone with a body that doesn't work properly? What is life like for them?

Explore the Bible

> He will wipe away all tears from their eyes. There will be no more death, no more grief or crying or pain. The old things have disappeared.
>
> *Revelation 21:4*

In this new heaven and earth that God has promised, everything will be perfect. It won't just be perfect because God will be living with us; it will be perfect for other reasons, too.

There will be no tears because there will be nothing to make us cry. No one will be in pain or die because everyone will be living for ever with God. We know that this will happen because God keeps his promises.

To do

Some of the feelings we have are bad or sad. However, there is always an opposite feeling that is good or happy. Here are some different faces.

Try to join up the opposites with a line.

Prayer jotter

Think about the things that make you cry and make you sad. Can you imagine that all those things will be gone?

Thank God for his promise of heaven, using this space here.

Signpost

Looking back

Is there anything that you are finding hard to do at the moment?

God cares. Tell him about it and ask him for his help.

To talk about

Have you ever been lost?

Do you know how to use a map? Have you ever had to use one? Do you remember a time when you and your family were looking out for a signpost to show you the way?

To do

Play this game either now or later. Send your friend out of the room and hide something somewhere in the room. Ask your friend to come back in and try to find it. Don't give any clues!

Now send your friend out again and hide the object again, somewhere else.

This time, when your friend comes back in, don't say exactly where the object is, but try to give directions to help him or her find it. For example, 'Go to the bed and go to the other side. Look under something blue…'

Explore the Bible

> **Jesus answered, 'I am the way, the truth, and the life; no one goes to the Father except by me.'**
>
> *John 14:6*

Jesus said that he was like a signpost or a map. He is the person who shows us the way to God. He promises that no one will find God without first looking to Jesus for directions.

It is important to find God because he gives us everything we need for life. We need to know Jesus as our friend so he can direct us to God.

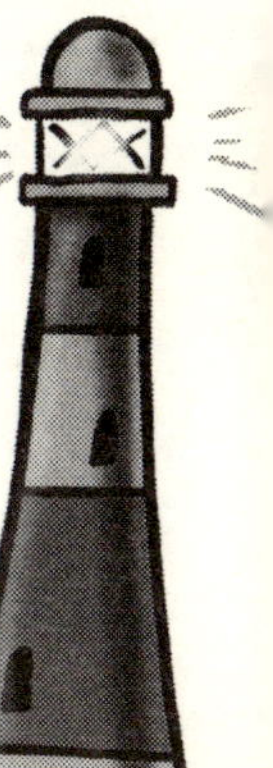

Prayer jotter

Here are some things that show us the way.

What does each one show the way to? Ask Jesus to keep showing you more about the way to God.

Big house

Looking back

What clubs or groups do you belong to? Thank God for them and what you do there.

Do you have a hobby? Thank God for that.

To talk about

Have you ever been to a building that has loads of rooms? Where was it? What is the building with the most number of rooms you can imagine? A skyscraper? A palace? A big school? Can you imagine what it would be like in a big building? Would you feel lost? Would you feel scared?

Explore the Bible

Do not be worried and upset. There are many rooms in my Father's house, and I am going to prepare a place for you.

John 14:1 and 2

Before Jesus went back to heaven, he talked to his disciples about what heaven was like. He told them it would be like a house with loads and loads of rooms. But this wasn't a big house for us to get lost in or feel lonely in.

Jesus promises that he is preparing a place for all his friends to go to. He is getting it all ready for when we go to be with him. So we don't need to be worried or scared, because heaven will be the best place ever.

To do

Here are some big buildings. But they haven't got any windows or doors. Can you draw them in? How many windows do you think they would have?

Prayer jotter

The Bible says that heaven will also be like one big party or banquet.

Imagine what it will be like from all you now know about heaven, and either write or draw about it here.

Heart hunger

Looking back

Think about what you did at school the last time you went. Thank God for what was good.

Ask him for help with something you find tricky.

To talk about

How do you feel when you have a really big meal? Have you ever had such a big meal that when it came to the next mealtime you were still not hungry? What's it like if you don't get enough to eat at a meal?

Have you ever been really thirsty? How do you know you need a drink? What does it feel like to drink a big glass of water?

Explore the Bible

> **Jesus said, 'I am the bread of life. Those who come to me will never be hungry; those who believe in me will never be thirsty.'**
>
> *John 6:35*

When Jesus says he is the 'bread of life', do you think he means that we can actually eat him?

No! He is talking about how he fills the hunger we have deep inside our hearts, not the hunger we have in our tummies. When he says we will never be thirsty, he doesn't mean that we will never need a drink again! He means that he will answer all our big questions about life.

At church, when we have a service of Holy Communion, people share bread and wine to remind each other that Jesus is the bread of life.

To do

Here are some plates of food and some drinks. Which would be your first choice if you were really hungry and thirsty? Is there something else you'd rather have? Draw it on the empty plate.

Prayer jotter

In some places in the world, people are very hungry—perhaps because the rain didn't water their plants, or because greedy rich people have taken all the food for themselves.

Pray that God will help those who are hungry to get food—food for their tummies, and food for their heart hunger.

Not full!

Looking back

What is your favourite animal? Why do you like it?

Thank God for the animal and why you like it.

To talk about

Have you ever been turned away because the place you wanted to go to was full up?

It might have been a bus, a swimming pool, a party or a shop. Can you think of another example?

What does it feel like to be turned away? Have you ever been on a waiting list for something—maybe for a club or a special activity? What is a waiting list for?

Explore the Bible

> **Everyone whom my Father gives me will come to me. I will never turn away anyone who comes to me.**
>
> *John 6:37*

Jesus promises that if we go to him for any reason, he will not turn us away. He can never be full, and he will never have a waiting list! God's love is so huge that there is enough room for everyone—including you and me!

To do

Are these places full or is there space?

Prayer jotter

Think of the things we go to Jesus for. Make a list or draw a picture of the things you think of.

Thank God that he always has room for us.

Friends

Looking back

What is the first thing you remember? Who was with you then?

God was with you then and even earlier. Thank him for always being there.

To talk about

What are friends like? When do you most like having friends around?

What do you most like doing with friends? What would life be like without friends?

To do

Circle some of the things here that you do with your friends:

Explore the Bible

> **The Helper will come—the Spirit, who reveals the truth about God and who comes from the Father. I will send him to you from the Father, and he will speak about me.**
>
> *John 15:26*

When Jesus went back to heaven, he promised his friends that he wouldn't leave them completely alone. He promised that he would send the Holy Spirit to come and be a friend and helper to them.

This friend isn't for playing on swings with. He is a deep-inside friend who is always there to remind us of all the things Jesus has taught us. He shows us how to live a life that pleases Jesus.

The Holy Spirit is a friend promised by God for everyone who knows Jesus. He helps us to work out what is good and bad, right and wrong.

Prayer jotter

Ask God to send his Holy Spirit to help you live a good life. Write or draw about our Holy Spirit friend here.

Always there

Looking back

What clothes did you wear in the day just gone? Have you clothes to wear tomorrow?

Thank God that you have clothes and shoes.

To talk about

Think of something you have had all your life. Have you got a toy that you were given when you were born? Or maybe a blanket or piece of clothing?

What about your hands? Have they stayed the same or changed? What about your nails and your hair?

Think of more things that stay the same and things that change.

Explore the Bible

Jesus said, 'I will be with you always, to the end of the age.'

Matthew 28:20

Jesus promises that he will always be with us. He will always be there, when we become an adult, if we ever become a parent, even if we become a grandparent. He will even be with us when this world finishes! That's a long time! And he won't change. He will be the same Jesus, always there, always caring for us.

He knows how we feel when we're sad as well as when we're happy.

To do

To help you remember this verse, only colour in the segments that have a dot in them.

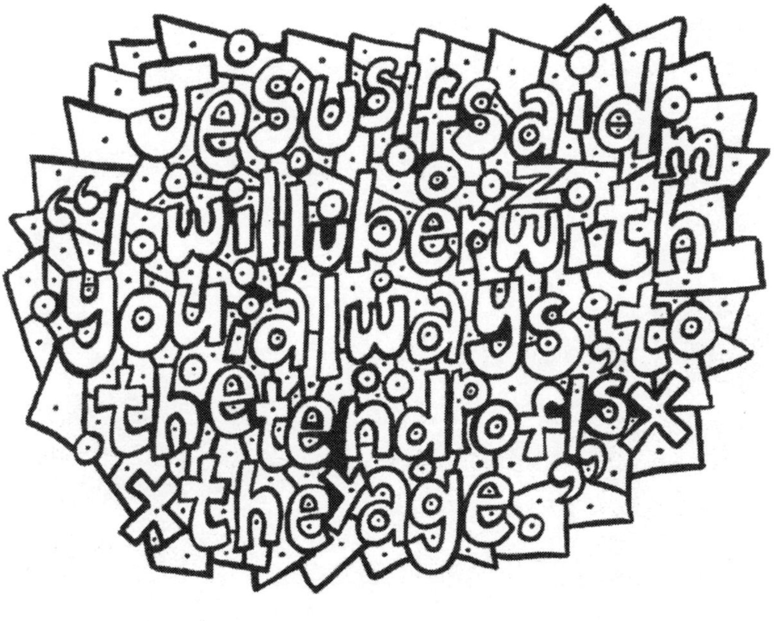

Prayer jotter

Do you ever feel lonely and scared? Remember that Jesus is with you!

Thank him for that. Draw yourself doing something scary and remember that Jesus is with you at that time.

The storm

Looking back

What can you see around you? What is inside? What is outside?

Thank God for all you have and everything he has made.

To talk about

Have you ever been out in a storm? Where were you? Were you outside or in a car? What was it like?

Have you ever seen a stormy sea? What was it like?

Explore the Bible

Suddenly a strong wind blew up, and the waves began to spill over into the boat. Jesus was sleeping with his head on a pillow. The disciples woke him up and said, 'Teacher, don't you care that we are about to die?'

Mark 4:37 and 38

Jesus and the disciples had had a very busy day. That evening they sailed across to the other side of Lake Galilee. Jesus was asleep at the back of the boat. Suddenly a storm blew up and the disciples were frightened.

What should they have done? What would you have done? They knew they were in danger and they knew Jesus would help them. But what happened next?

To do

Put these pictures in the right order to re-tell the story so far.

Prayer jotter

When you get really worried about something, do you ask God to help? Think of the times when you might suddenly need God's help or when you really need to know he is there.

Write or draw about it here.

Calm again

Looking back

Is there anyone you know who isn't well at the moment? Pray for God to be with them.

Pray for the doctors and nurses who look after people who are unwell.

To talk about

Who do you turn to for help? It might be an older brother or sister, a parent or a friend.

When might you need their help? Do you trust them to make things OK?

Explore the Bible

Jesus stood up and commanded the wind, 'Be quiet!' and he said to the waves, 'Be still!' The wind died down, and there was a great calm. Then Jesus said to his disciples, 'Why are you frightened? Have you still no faith?'

Mark 4:39 and 40

The disciples were in a real panic! They thought the boat was going to sink. And Jesus was asleep. Did he not care? They shook Jesus to wake him. 'Help!' they cried.

Jesus got up and told the sea and the wind to calm down. They did. But then he asked the disciples why they had panicked. Surely they knew Jesus would save them.

Sometimes life feels very frightening. But Jesus wants us to trust in him so much that we don't panic. He knows what we're going through and will help us.

To do

Finish putting the pictures for the story in the right order.

Prayer jotter

Sometimes life feels a bit stormy—things might suddenly feel difficult. At other times life is calm and everything is going along just fine.

God is interested in our life however it feels. How does life feel at the moment? Tell God and ask him to give you what you need for now.

Confidence in Jesus

Looking back

Is there anything you are looking forward to at the moment? Why are you looking forward to it?

Thank God for it.

To talk about

How confident are you?

Being confident means that you are sure of something before you even try it. For example, are you confident that you know your alphabet? Are you confident that you know how to spell your address?

Sometimes we're not very sure, sometimes we're totally confident.

To do

Which of these things would you be confident of doing?

Explore the Bible

Jairus, an official of the local synagogue, arrived, and when he saw Jesus, he threw himself down at his feet and begged him earnestly, 'My little daughter is very ill. Please come and place your hands on her, so that she will get well and live!'

Mark 5:22 and 23

Jairus' little girl was very ill. No doctor could make her better. In fact, she was getting worse. But Jairus knew how she could get better. He would ask Jesus. Jesus could make her better. Jairus had so much faith in Jesus. He had confidence that Jesus could make his daughter well again.

When you pray to God, do you have confidence that he will answer your prayer? God wants us to ask him with confidence, knowing that he loves us and grants the answer that we need to our prayers.

Prayer jotter

Talk to God now, knowing that he will answer you.

Draw something from today's session.

Week 4
Session 4

Too late

Looking back

Say sorry to God for the things that people in the world do that upset him. They might not be things you have done yourself, like pollution or war, but they still upset him.

To talk about

What does it feel like when something you've been doing doesn't go to plan? When has this happened to you?

How do you feel when, in the middle of doing something, things start going wrong?

To do

Can you see what has gone wrong in these pictures?

Explore the Bible

Messengers came from Jairus' house and told him, 'Your daughter has died.' Jesus said, 'Don't be afraid, only believe.' He took her by the hand and said, 'Little girl, I tell you to get up!' She got up at once and started walking around.

Mark 5:35–36 and 41–42

Jairus' plan suddenly changed. He knew that Jesus could make his daughter well again. But now she had died. They were too late! Jairus was really upset. But Jesus told him to carry on believing—it wasn't too late! Jesus went and brought the little girl back to life. He made the impossible happen.

Sometimes we might think that everything has gone wrong and there is no hope. But, with Jesus, we can always have hope and always believe. He makes the impossible possible.

Prayer jotter

What wonderful good news it was that Jairus believed Jesus could help him. His confidence in Jesus was proved right.

We will never understand how Jesus answers our prayers, but we must believe he does.

Draw or write about something from today's session.

Secrets

Looking back

Do you like books? Do you like reading? Do you find reading easy or hard?

Talk to God about books and reading. Ask him to help you if you need it.

To talk about

Have you ever kept a secret? Don't tell what it is if it's still secret!

Do you know the difference between a good secret and a bad one? Do you think you can keep secrets from God?

To do

These people have a secret. Unfortunately, they have left a clue on themselves. Can you work out their secret?

Explore the Bible

> There was a woman who had suffered terribly from severe bleeding for twelve years. She had heard about Jesus, so she came in the crowd behind him, saying to herself, 'If I just touch his clothes, I will get well.'
>
> *Mark 5:25, 27 and 28*

The lady in this story had a secret. She had been ill for twelve years. No doctor could help her. She had almost given up hope of getting better.

In those days, her illness meant that no one was allowed to talk to her, so she kept out of people's way. But she knew that Jesus would be able to heal her, if only she could touch him. But, because no one was allowed to talk to her, she had to do it in secret.

Do you think Jesus will notice?

Prayer jotter

Is there anything we can keep secret from God?

He knows everything about us. This might feel strange at first, but because God loves us so much, he would never use our secrets in a bad way, only for our good.

If you are worried about something you have been told to keep secret, it is probably best to talk to someone you trust. They will help you to know if it is a good or bad secret.

Week 4
Session 6

Ill for ages

Looking back

Have you heard any good news recently? What was it? Thank God for it.

To talk about

Do you know anyone who has been ill for a long time? Some people have an illness that stays with them all their life. Some people get ill during their life and are ill for a while. Talk about illness, what it is like and how it must feel.

Explore the Bible

She touched his cloak, and her bleeding stopped at once. Jesus knew that power had gone out of him, so he asked, 'Who touched my clothes?' The woman realized what had happened to her, so she came and told him the whole truth. Jesus said, 'My daughter, your faith has made you well.'

Mark 5:29–30 and 33–34

The woman who had touched Jesus' cloak was made better. But her secret was out. Jesus had realized what had happened when his healing power went out of his body.

Jesus told the woman that it was her faith in his ability to heal her that had made her better. She was now free to live a normal life.

To do

Here is a picture of the woman trying secretly to touch Jesus' cloak. Think about the story and colour the picture if you like.

Prayer jotter

Pray for the people you know who are unwell. Jesus can make everyone well again. But sometimes getting completely well doesn't happen until we are in heaven. If this is the case, we need Jesus to make us well enough to be happy as we are.

Write or draw your thoughts here.

Jobs

Looking back

Is there anything sad happening in the world at the moment? Pray for the people affected, that God will give them what they need.

To talk about

What jobs do the adults you know do? Have you ever asked people about their jobs? What does their job mean that they do? Do they wear a uniform? What job would you like to have when you grow up?

Explore the Bible

As Jesus walked along the shore of Lake Galilee, he saw two fishermen, Simon and his brother Andrew, catching fish with a net. Jesus said to them, 'Come with me, and I will teach you to catch people.' At once they left their nets and went with him.

Mark 1:16–18

Simon and Andrew were fishermen. They spent all their time on a boat catching fish, whatever the weather. Imagine what that job is like. I bet they smelt of fish all the time!

Jesus came along and asked them to join him. They had never met Jesus before. But they must have been very sure that Jesus was special because they left their jobs immediately and followed him.

How did they know? Maybe they didn't know. Maybe they just had faith.

To do

Jesus said that the fishermen would start catching people instead of fish. How many fish and how many people are there in this net?

Prayer jotter

Think of one of the people you talked about earlier. Draw them doing their job and pray for them at work.

Week 5
Session 2

Names

Looking back

What are your favourite toys?

Some children have no toys. Pray for them. Ask God to show you if there is anything you can do to help.

To talk about

Do you know that most names have a meaning behind them? Do you know what yours means?

Most surnames originally came from the job people did. Mr Baker was the man who made the bread. Nowadays that isn't so. Talk about why you were called what you were. Were you called after someone? Is it a family name? Is it your grandmother's name?

Names are important. It really hurts people when we use bad names for them and it makes them feel good when we call them good names.

To do

In the old days, people's names meant their job. Can you draw a line between the people and the things of their job?

Mr Baker | Mrs Potter | Charlie Butcher | Paul Green

Explore the Bible

Jesus looked at Simon and said, 'Your name is Simon son of John, but you will be called Cephas.' (This is the same as Peter and means 'a rock'.)

John 1:42

Jesus and Simon became good friends after their first meeting on the beach. Jesus decided that Simon needed to change his name. He decided to call him Peter because this suited what Simon was like. Jesus thought he was like a rock—solid and reliable.

Prayer jotter

Think of the good names you have heard for God and for Jesus. Ask an adult who knows, if you need some help. Make a list or draw a picture of yourself praising God using his names.

All of a sudden

Looking back

What is your favourite television programme?

Thank God for the good things on television.

To talk about

Has anyone ever dared you to do something? To climb to the top of the climbing-frame? To dive from the board at the swimming-pool?

Have you ever dared someone to do something? Were you able to do it? What was it like? Is there anything you didn't dare do?

Explore the Bible

Jesus came, walking on the water. Peter spoke up. 'Lord, if it is really you, order me to come out on the water to you.' 'Come!' answered Jesus. So Peter got out and started walking to Jesus. But when he noticed the strong wind, he was afraid and started to sink…

Matthew 14:25, 28–30

Sometimes we decide all of a sudden that something is a good thing to do. That is what Peter was like. He suddenly felt so sure that Jesus could help him walk on the water. And he did. Peter walked on the water. Quite an impossible thing to do!

But suddenly Peter noticed the waves. He stopped looking at Jesus and started to sink. He had faith enough to step on to water, but not enough to hold him there. Poor Peter!

To do

Here is a picture of Peter walking on the water for you to colour.

Prayer jotter

How much do you trust Jesus? Is there anything you want him to help you to do, even if it feels impossible?

Write it or draw it here and then talk to an adult you trust about why you want to do it.

Special friend

Looking back

What is your church like? Thank God for the people there.

Pray that your church leaders will do their job well and help people to know God better.

To talk about

Have you ever been let down by a friend? Why did they not stand up for you? What did it feel like?

Have you ever let a friend down?

To do

Good friends are very special. We need to make sure they know how special they are to us.

Make a card to give to your special friends to tell them how good it is being their friend.

Explore the Bible

> Peter said, 'I swear that I am telling the truth! I do not know the man you are talking about!' Just then a cock crowed a second time, and Peter remembered how Jesus had said to him, 'Before the cock crows twice, you will say three times that you do not know me.' And he broke down and cried.
>
> *Mark 14:71–72*

Peter was one of Jesus' best friends. But despite being such a good friend, when Jesus needed his help he let him down.

When Jesus was arrested, Peter was asked if he knew Jesus. Instead of saying, 'Yes, he's one of my best friends' he told three different people that he had never met Jesus before.

Poor Peter! To make things worse, Jesus had told him beforehand that he would deny their friendship. As the cock crowed, Peter remembered Jesus' words and burst into tears.

Prayer jotter

Is there anything you have done to a friend that hurt them? Sometimes we need to say sorry, even if the thing happened ages ago.

Think about this and ask God to give you the courage to say sorry.

Ask God to help you to be a really good friend. Draw your friends here.

Checking up

Looking back

Have you seen anyone upset and crying in the past few days? Why were they crying?

If they are still sad, pray that God will be with them.

To talk about

Have you ever been so unsure of someone that you had to keep checking about something? Does anyone keep asking you the same question to make sure you have remembered something?

Sometimes it is good to be reminded of things, but sometimes we get tired of it. When do people check up on you?

To do

Here are some people checking things. Can you think of any more people who check things?

Explore the Bible

A third time Jesus said, 'Simon son of John, do you love me?' Peter was sad because Jesus asked him the third time, so he said, 'Lord, you know everything; you know that I love you!'

John 21:17

Peter and Jesus were good friends, but Peter had told three people that he didn't know Jesus. This must have hurt Jesus.

Our Bible verse today takes place after Jesus had died and come back to life. He wanted to be sure that Peter really did love him. Jesus asked Peter three times if he loved him. This was the same number of times that Peter had denied knowing Jesus. Peter said 'yes' each time. He really did love Jesus and wanted him to know it.

Prayer jotter

Jesus wants to know that you love him. Have you told him lately?

Tell him now and draw a picture to show him that you love him.

What a difference!

Looking back

What is your favourite food? Why do you like it? When did you last have it?

Thank God for food and that we have tastebuds to taste it.

To talk about

Have you ever seen people change the way they are? Sometimes they change because their mood changes. Sometimes people change because they have learnt to do something new.

Who have you seen change?

To do

Here are some things that change from one thing to something else. Match them up.

Explore the Bible

Then Peter stood up with the other eleven apostles and in a loud voice began to speak to the crowd. Many of them believed his message and were baptized, and about 3,000 people were added to the group that day.

Acts 2:14 and 41

Peter changed amazingly! We saw him being so unsure of his friendship with Jesus that he said he didn't know him. Now we see Peter so sure about Jesus that he is able to stand up and tell 3,000 people how great Jesus is. What a change!

Because Peter believed in Jesus, the crowd believed too. What a difference believing in Jesus makes to people!

Prayer jotter

Jesus made a difference to Peter's life. And he wants to make a difference to your life, too.

Write or draw something here about the difference believing in God makes to our lives.